Immigration

Philip Brooks

Heinemann Library
Chicago, Illinois

Designed by Herman Adler Design
Printed in the United States by Lake Book Manufacturing, Inc.

08 07 06 05 04
10 9 8 7 6 5 4 3 2 1

Library of Congress Cataloging-in-Publication Data
Brooks, Philip, 1963–
  Immigration / Philip Brooks.
      p. cm. — (20th-century perspectives)
Summary: A historical account of immigration to the United States since
the arrival of the Mayflower, discussing reasons why various groups left
their homelands, and dispelling myths behind some common prejudices
toward immigrants.
Includes bibliographical references and index.
  ISBN 1-4034-3807-2 (lib. bdg. hardcover) — ISBN 1-4034-4181-2 (pbk.)
  1. United States—Emigration and immigration—Juvenile literature. [1.
United States—Emigration and immigration—History. 2.
Immigrants—United States—History.] I. Title. II. Series.

  JV6465.B62 2003
  304.8'73—dc21
                              2003009559

Acknowledgments
The author and publisher are grateful to the following for permission to reproduce copyright material:
pp. 4, 8 Corbis; p. 6 North Wind Pictures; pp. 7, 8, 18, 19 Hulton Deutsch Collection/Corbis; pp. 10, 11,
12, 15, 16, 17, 21, 23, 26 Bettmann/Corbis; p. 13 Hulton Archive by Getty Images; p. 14 Underwood &
Underwood/Corbis; p. 20 Porfirian Fedualism by Juan O'Gorman/Archivo Iconographico, S.A./Corbis;
p. 22 Culver Pictures; p. 24 Time Magazine ©Time Inc./.Timepix/Getty Images; pp. 25, 27(t), 36,
37, 40 AP/Wide World; pp. 27(b), 28, 33 AFP/Corbis; p. 29 Nathan Benn/Corbis; p. 30 Spencer Grant/
PhotoEdit; p. 31 Michael Newman/PhotoEdit; p. 32 Getty Images: pp. 34, 35 David Howells/Corbis;
p. 38 John Nordell/2001© The Christian Science Monitor; p. 39 Yolanda Zambrano; p. 41 A. Ramey/
PhotoEdit; p. 42 Richard Hamilton Smith/Corbis; p. 43 Najlah Feanny/Corbis

Cover photo reproduced with permission of Bettman/Corbis

Every effort has been made to contact copyright holders of any material reproduced in this book. Any
omissions will be rectified in subsequent printings if notice is given to the publisher.

Contents

Introduction

Coming to America

From the 1600s, people worldwide have traveled long and far to gain freedom and opportunity in the United States. Countless waves of newcomers to the United States strengthened the nation and helped secure the basic rights listed in the Declaration of Independence. They have built the United States into the strongest nation in the world.

The history of immigration is difficult, though. Native-born Americans have not always welcomed immigrants. Some Americans have warned against allowing each new wave of immigration, whether it came from Europe, Africa, or Asia. However, worries and predictions of danger have always proven false. Each wave of immigration has improved the nation.

About the same number of immigrants came from England as Africa. But there was a difference: Africans were forced to come as slaves.

PRE-1790 IMMIGRATION	
Country/Region	Number Immigrated
African	300,000
English	300,000
Scotch-Irish	100,000
German	100,000
Scottish	75,000

Immigrants first came to the United States seeking freedom to practice their chosen religion. Today, immigrants are more likely to be escaping political trouble in their home country. Others come because they believe the U.S. is a place where those willing to work hard can live well and get rich.

Living in a wilderness

Long before written histories were kept, North America was a huge wilderness. Scientists believe that the first humans in North America came from Asia more than 20,000 years ago. These newcomers moved south. They are the ancestors of American Indian tribes that spread across what would become Canada, the United States, Mexico, and Central and South America.

Thousands of years later, explorers from Europe and Scandinavia arrived in what they called "the New World." The Spanish established their first settlement in present-day Florida in 1565 and later created other settlements in Texas and California.

Slavery: immigrants in chains

In order to farm in the New World, British, Dutch, and Spanish settlers needed labor. The British began sending criminals to the New World to provide the labor needed to clear land and build settlements. They finished their sentences and then were free. Other would-be immigrants paid for passage to the New World by promising five to seven years of labor to a sponsor. Such laborers were often abused. They became restless and demanded improved conditions. Many escaped before their term of work was finished.

Early settlers solved this problem by capturing people from Africa and the Caribbean to be slaves in the New World. Slaves worked in Virginia fields as early as 1619. These forced immigrants eased the labor shortage, but they bothered the conscience of a nation supposedly founded on the idea that all people "were created equal" and deserved "life, liberty, and the pursuit of happiness."

Negroes for Sale.

A Cargo of very fine stout Men and Women, in good order and fit for immediate service, just imported from the Windward Coast of Africa, in the Ship Two Brothers.— Conditions are one half Cash or Produce, the other half payable the first of January next, giving Bond and Security if required.

The Sale to be opened at 10 o'Clock each Day, in Mr. Bourdeaux's Yard, at No. 48, on the Bay. May 19, 1784. JOHN MITCHELL.

Thirty Seasoned Negroes

To be Sold for Credit, at Private Sale.

AMONGST which is a Carpenter, none of whom are known to be dishonest.

Also, to be sold for Cash, a regular bred young Negroe Man-Cook, born in this Country, who served several Years under an exceeding good French Cook abroad, and his Wife a middle aged Washer-Woman, (both very honest) and their two Children. Likewise, a young Man a Carpenter.

For Terms apply to the Printer.

This 1784 advertisement for a slave auction was not an uncommon sight in the United States in the 1700s.

In the 1600s, British people desiring greater religious freedom rode ships on dangerous three-month journeys across the Atlantic to start colonies in what are now New England and Virginia. Dutch adventurers founded New Amsterdam on the island of Manhattan, which they purchased from American Indians in 1626. Immigrants from Sweden started a colony in Delaware around the same time.

These newcomers encountered American Indian tribes. Sometimes relations between the two were friendly. But much of the story of the early United States includes the destruction of American Indian life. Conflict occurred, especially as the Europeans spread across the country. But more deadly were diseases the Europeans carried, such as smallpox. Tribes shrank dramatically. By the 1840s, this coast-to-coast takeover was called "Manifest Destiny" by many whites. Today, many people agree that what was done to American Indians in the quest for more and more land amounts to genocide.

The U.S. government broke treaty after treaty and drove many tribes into near extinction through forced marches to bare reservations with few resources. In addition, the buffalo, the main source of food and materials for many tribes, was systematically hunted and destroyed. This forced American Indians to abandon tribal lands or face starvation. Even today, many American Indians suffer from poverty and poor education.

Who can be citizens

One of the first acts of the United States Congress was to pass the Naturalization Act in 1790. " . . . Any alien, being a free white person, may be admitted to become a citizen of the United States," the law said.

During the 1790s, French colonists fleeing a revolt in Haiti immigrated to the United States. Then, from the late 1790s through the very early 1800s, about 6000 people each year took advantage of the Naturalization Act to become citizens.

The same session of Congress decided to count the nation's people in an official census. In 1790, the population of the United States was about 3.9 million. Almost 20 percent of that population was African slaves and their children. In 1808, Congress banned the slave trade, meaning slaves could no longer be imported from Africa. Although there would be no more forced immigrants, their offspring remained slaves.

A hand-colored woodcut from the 1500s shows a ship of the kind that brought many immigrants to the territory that would become the United States.

Wars slow immigration

Several wars soon slowed the pace of immigration. In 1806, France fought Great Britain. Their powerful warring navies disturbed shipping and passage across the Atlantic. The War of 1812 between Great Britain and the United States also greatly reduced emigration from Europe. U.S. victory in 1814 set off the first massive wave of immigration to the United States.

At different times in the 1800s, the port cities of New York, Boston, Philadelphia, and Charleston were overwhelmed with newcomers from Germany, Italy, Great Britain, Mexico, Canada, and the Caribbean. Many immigrants were sick from long journeys on overcrowded, undersupplied ships. It took Congress a long time to respond to this health and safety problem. In 1890, it eventually

passed the Steerage Act, which required ship captains to keep better records on passengers and made them responsible for the health and safety of travelers and crew.

The Industrial Revolution

During the late 1700s and early 1800s, life was changed in huge ways by rapid advances in methods of manufacturing and farming. This "Industrial Revolution" included the invention of better and cheaper machinery for planting, harvesting, and processing. Fewer people were necessary to farm larger and larger areas of land. Between 1760 and 1830, many English peasants whose families had worked as farmers for centuries found themselves pushed off their land. In industry, improved weaving machines reduced by 80 percent the number of workers needed to turn wool into yarn. These events spread throughout Europe, leaving many people without jobs.

A ship-building shop in England in 1867 shows the kind of hard work and conditions common after the Industrial Revolution. Many Europeans immigrated to the United States to get their own land and find more opportunities.

Opportunity in the United States

Many farmers went to European cities to work and when the cities had no more jobs, many looked to the United States. While Europe found fewer uses for its laborers and farmers, the United States was growing rapidly and needed all the help it could get. Good economic times in general led to friendly conditions for immigrants to the United States. With cities like Chicago and St. Louis just beginning to rise out of the prairie, anyone willing to work was welcome. By 1864, President Abraham Lincoln's Republican Party would include the following in its platform: "Foreign immigration which in the past has added so much to the wealth, resources, and increase of power to the nation . . . should be . . . encouraged."

Lincoln had another reason to welcome immigrants during the Civil War. Most of them settled in the north and eventually fought on the Union side. Italian, Irish, and German immigrants were important in winning the war. French, Scottish, and Scandinavian troops also fought on the northern side. During the Civil War, the United States also encouraged immigration as a way to fill jobs left by soldiers and to put pro-Union citizens in underpopulated states such as Illinois, Indiana, and Missouri.

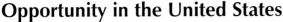

The Irish Come, 1846–1850

Spoiled crops

The Irish Potato Famine which started in the mid–1840s eventually killed nearly one million people and left millions more sickened and hungry. About 1.5 million Irish people emigrated to the United States and helped reshape both nations.

The famine began with a disease called the potato blight that attacked potatoes and other crops. Potatoes were the main source of food for Irish peasants and laborers. Farmers ate what they could grow and lived in poverty even in good times. But too many Irish relied on the potato for survival. Ireland was a colony of Great Britain at the time, and although it produced enough food besides potatoes to feed its people,

This 1849 drawing shows Irish Famine victims receiving help. Conditions became so bad that many Irish decided they had to leave Ireland.

much of it was sold to England. Across Ireland, the horrible smell of rotting potatoes hung over farmers' fields. But British authorities offered little assistance as conditions grew worse and worse.

Ireland's landlords were also a problem. They were mostly Protestant and of English descent, and they charged high rents to poor, mostly Catholic farmers. As the disease began affecting harvests across Europe, food became more scarce, and as it became more scarce, it grew more expensive. Desperate peasants began eating rotted fruits and vegetables, and many got sick and died from typhus and cholera. The year 1847 is often called "Black '47" by the Irish. Death from disease and starvation had become so common and money so short that the Irish were forced to bury many victims without coffins.

Death and desperation

An estimated 500,000 Irish peasant farmers who could not pay their rent were evicted. A few of the evicted burned their property or even murdered landlords and their agents. Most gathered in overcrowded city workhouses where conditions were terribly unhealthy. Those who could afford tickets took crowded ships to the United States. Between death and emigration, the population of Ireland fell from 8 million to 5 million in the mid-1800s.

Most of these new immigrants went to New York City. Others traveled to cities such as Philadelphia, Pittsburgh, and Boston. By 1850, one out of every five residents of Boston and New York City was an Irish immigrant. Gradually, Irish in New York City and Boston would be accepted and gain political strength. Also, Irish immigrant labor became important in laying the eastern half of the transcontinental railroad system, which was finished in 1869. Chinese labor would contribute greatly to the building of the western leg.

This is Boston, Massachussetts in 1859. In only ten years, Boston's Irish population had grown to become 20 percent of the population.

Creating stereotypes overlooks injustice

"Nativists" were Americans in the mid-1800s who wanted immigration limited or eliminated. They grew uncomfortable with this flood of immigrants, and the Irish were the target of prejudice. As nativists and Irish-Americans began to clash, stereotypes about Irish people appeared. They were characterized as stupid, wicked, lazy, and drunk. It was thought the men liked to fight and were mean. Women were stereotyped as being hardworking but simpleminded, likely to waste money on lazy husbands and relatives as well as giving birth to countless children. Such nasty stereotypes helped longer-established Americans overlook the terrible conditions under which many new, poor Irish immigrants lived and worked.

China Comes to California

The first Chinese immigrants arrived in California in 1820. But when news of the California gold rush reached China around 1850, thousands packed their few belongings and crossed the ocean in hopes of finding riches.

Skilled miners

Many Chinese who came were skilled miners and brought some improved techniques. They built devices such as waterwheels for power, "rockers" that sifted large amounts of soil and sand in search of gold nuggets, and a bucket-and-pulley system that dredged river bottoms where larger nuggets were hidden. Chinese mining camps were also extremely well organized and self-sufficient, necessary because of prejudice from white miners. While American miners accepted English-speaking Europeans and occasionally tolerated Latin Americans, they usually treated the Chinese badly. Most maddening to white miners was that Chinese miners were very skilled at taking over abandoned mines and making them valuable.

Not all white miners were cruel to the Chinese. The largest Chinese mining camp, known as Chinese Camp, was established with the help of sympathetic white miners. However, even during the peak of the California gold rush, few individual miners, American or foreign, actually became rich. Frustration grew, and white miners began to blame the Chinese for creating too much competition.

In 1850, the California legislature adopted a Foreign Miners License Law, charging all non-U.S. miners twenty dollars per month. The high fee caused many Chinese to quit mining for gold. They moved to San Francisco and soon found work in the city's business community, helping to create America's first "Chinatown," which is still lively today.

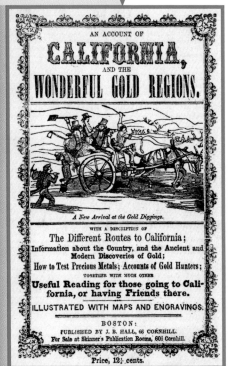

AN ACCOUNT OF

CALIFORNIA,
AND THE
WONDERFUL GOLD REGIONS.

A New Arrival at the Gold Diggings.

WITH A DESCRIPTION OF

The Different Routes to California;
Information about the Country, and the Ancient and Modern Discoveries of Gold;
How to Test Precious Metals; Accounts of Gold Hunters;
TOGETHER WITH MUCH OTHER

Useful Reading for those going to California, or having Friends there.

ILLUSTRATED WITH MAPS AND ENGRAVINGS.

BOSTON:
PUBLISHED BY J. B. HALL, 66 CORNHILL.
For Sale at Skinner's Publication Rooms, 60½ Cornhill.

Price, 12½ cents.

"The Chinese must go!"

Stories of mistreatment in California did little to discourage Chinese immigration. In 1852, of the 67,000 immigrants who flocked to California in hopes of becoming rich, 20,000 came from China.

By 1860, the census listed 70 percent of all Chinese in the United States as miners, nearly all of them in California. The West would soon need their labor. In 1863 work began on the Central Pacific Railroad. The line ran east from Sacramento and eventually connected in Utah with the Union Pacific Railroad being built from the east.

More than 10,000 Chinese laborers laid track and built bridges and trestles. It took physical courage, brilliant engineering, and imagination to meet the challenges of laying track across the western wilderness. Chinese workers also became experts at handling the dangerous dynamite needed to blast routes through the Sierra Mountains. In spite of their importance in linking the country, the Chinese still suffered from prejudice.

63,000 Chinese lived in the United States by 1870. When economic trouble hit California during the 1870s, an anti-Chinese movement was begun by a man named Denis Kearney. Kearney created the Workingmen's Party of California in 1877, whose cry was "the Chinese must go."

Workers celebrate the meeting of the Union Pacific and Central Pacific Railroads at Promontory Point, Utah, in 1869. Chinese labor was essential to the western half of the effort.

Kearney and others feared that the Chinese would overwhelm the nation and take jobs away from "natives." Congress eventually passed the Chinese Exclusion Act in 1882. The law banned Chinese from coming to the United States. They were the only group ever selected for such treatment. Obvious differences in language, culture, and physical appearance made them easy targets for racists.

The first Chinese laundry

Chinese entrepreneurs saw that most miners had no way to clean their clothes. Doing laundry would be a way to make a living with little equipment or money. Only a trough, water, ironing board, and iron were necessary. Many historians believe that a man named Wah Lee opened the first full-service laundry in San Francisco in 1851. He charged two dollars to wash and iron a dozen men's shirts. Chinese laundries spread across the country. 30 percent of Chinese by 1920 listed their job as laundry work.

"Know-Nothings" Against Catholics and Immigrants

Waves of Catholics

More than two million Catholics from Ireland and Germany came to the United States in the first half of the 1800s. Their arrival caused a hostile response from some native-born Protestant Americans. Many Protestants disliked the different customs immigrants brought with them from their homelands. Even worse, they thought, immigrants competed for jobs in eastern cities such as New York, Boston, and Baltimore.

Changes in politics helped immigrants, too. During the 1820s and 1830s many states changed their constitutions to give every white male the right to vote. This meant that European immigrants now had political power. Many longtime city leaders—native-born Americans—were defeated in elections that included these thousands of new voters. Finally, the Catholic Church failed to support the anti-alcohol, or temperance, movement. This made some Protestants think that the Vatican, the Catholic headquarters in Rome, Italy, hoped to weaken the social fabric of the United States with alcohol.

This illustration shows a torchlight meeting of the Know-Nothings, held in New York City in 1855 in front of City Hall.

The rise of the Know-Nothings

Various so-called "nativist" organizations appeared that aimed to keep immigrants down. One calling itself the Order of the Star-Spangled Banner was founded in 1849 as a secret society. When members were asked questions about the group, they would say they knew nothing about it. For this reason, they soon came to be called the "Know-Nothings."

Know-Nothings hoped to extend the residency period required for a person to become a U.S. citizen from five to twenty-one years. They also sought to legally forbid the foreign-born and Catholics from holding public office.

Among the oaths taken by members of the Know-Nothing Party was a promise never to vote for a Roman Catholic. The party did become politically strong for a short time. At its peak, the party claimed 1.5 million voters and won city elections in Baltimore, Washington, and Philadelphia. At least 40 Congressmen from six states were at one time associated with the Know-Nothings. In 1854, Know-Nothings held both houses of the state legislature of Massachusetts and also ran strong campaigns in Delaware and New York.

Anti-immigrant activity was not limited to politics. In Louisville, Kentucky, a Know-Nothing celebration was held on election day, August 6, 1855. It grew into a riot, 25 Irish-Americans were killed, and the Louisville Roman Catholic cathedral was damaged. Louisville's Catholic Church claimed that the mayor and police had done nothing to stop the rioters: " . . . City authorities, all Know-Nothings, looked calmly on, and they are now endeavoring to lay the blame on the Catholics," wrote church officials.

This is piano sheet music for a Know-Nothing song. In an attempt to say that Know-Nothingism was patriotic, the song's words described how "Citizen Know-Nothing" was "Uncle Sam's youngest son."

The Know-Nothing Party finally split along Northern and Southern lines before the Civil War and never regained its strength.

Anti-Catholics try to kill Pope's messenger

The riot in Kentucky was not a rare event. In 1853, the Pope sent Archbishop Bedini to the United States to help settle legal questions about some church properties in Philadelphia and Buffalo. The highest-ranking Catholic official ever to come to the United States, Bedini became the target of a failed murder attempt in New York City, and Cincinnati, Ohio.

In Cincinnati, a violent mob gathered outside the Roman Catholic cathedral with the intention of killing Bedini. After police shot and wounded several of his would-be killers, Bedini escaped the United States in secret.

Ellis and Angel Islands

By the mid-1800s, steam-powered ships made ocean passage safer and cheaper. Immigrants poured into the United States as Europeans and Scandinavians especially were welcomed. Nine percent of Norway's population came in the second half of the 1800s. Between 1880 and 1930, 27 million immigrants came to the United States.

Ellis Island, gateway for millions

If you are of European descent, your ancestors probably passed through Ellis Island Immigration Station, which opened in New York in 1892. The Statue of Liberty in New York Harbor was a hopeful sight for them. But the next step, being admitted, could be an anxious process. Upon leaving a ship with their few belongings, new arrivals were sent to the Registry Room. There, doctors examined them for diseases such as tuberculosis.

Immigrants wait in line in the Registry Room at Ellis Island in 1912.

Immigrants with health problems that required treatment but not a denial of entrance were sent to the infirmary. Agents also checked identification papers. Although the overwhelming majority of immigrants at Ellis Island were admitted, such inspections probably made them briefly worry that they would be sent back home.

By 1924, Ellis Island had admitted 75 percent of all immigrants who came to the United States. At its peak, Ellis Island had 700 workers processing up to 5,000 immigrants per day. The station had a hospital, restaurant, bathhouse, and laundry. Immigration slowed greatly during World War I, and Ellis Island was used mainly to imprison captured German sailors and suspected alien enemies.

In 1990, Ellis Island was reopened as the National Immigration Museum.

Family help

Many immigrants were met by family members who had immigrated before them. Families often first sent one or two men to the United States who earned money to bring others. All then helped pay for still more relatives.

Angel Island

If Ellis Island represented a gateway, San Francisco's Angel Island, established in 1910, often acted more like a closed gate. One in every six Asians attempting to enter the United States was sent home.

The Chinese Exclusion Act of 1882 practically eliminated Chinese immigration, but the United States could not keep out all Chinese immigrants. At the time, if a person's father was a U.S. citizen, so was that person. Many Chinese immigrants created what came to be called a "paper son" or "paper daughter" by simply claiming to have children still in China. They then sold or gave false papers naming incoming immigrants as their children.

First arrivals at Ellis and Angel

Of the hundreds of thousands of immigrants who were processed at Ellis Island, the first was Annie Moore of Ireland. She received a handshake, greetings, and a ten-dollar gold piece from the U.S. Immigration Commissioner.

Angel Island's first arrival, a Chinese man named Lin, was not so lucky. He was detained and on his cell walls he wrote about being arrested and imprisoned.

This is a 1935 photo of Angel Island. Through this station, thousands of immigrants from China, Japan, and other Asian countries passed through or were detained as they tried to enter the United States.

Paper sons or daughters hoping to enter the United States in this way memorized the family information listed on their documentation. Angel Island inspectors knew that such dishonesty was widespread and often questioned Asians for hours to find lies that would result in their rejection. Ellis Island was different. Inspectors there rarely barred immigrants for reasons other than health.

Following interviews and investigations, Asian immigrants often were detained for a month, as they waited to learn whether or not they would be admitted into the United States. Angel Island's living conditions were awful. The wooden barracks were dirty and unhealthful. One official called the place "an outrage to civilization." Those waiting sometimes wrote poetry on the barracks walls, describing their troubles. Many poems carved then can still be seen today. Others were copied by two detainees, Smiley Jann and Tet Yee, in 1931–1932.

The complex today is the Angel Island Immigration Museum.

America Closes Its Door, 1920s and 1930s

Immigration to the United States changed between 1920 and the late 1930s, the period between World War I and World War II. Difficult economic times, combined with new distrust of foreigners, led to prejudice. People worried that immigrants from countries with communists or socialists would threaten United States capitalism. They believed that immigration threatened the nation's strength and its way of life.

Eugenics, false science for prejudice

Organizations such as the Immigration Restriction League worked to reduce the number of new immigrants admitted. Many of the reasons given were based on the false science of eugenics.

This is Calvin Coolidge, U.S. president from 1923 to 1929. He placed stricter controls on immigration.

In 1920, a man named Harry Laughlin appeared before the U.S. House of Representatives Committee on Immigration and Naturalization. Using census information and a survey of the number of foreign-born people in prisons, he argued that immigrants could "pollute" the American people. He claimed that scientific evidence showed that many eastern and southern European immigrants were mentally and morally undesirable. The Public Health Service, responsible for medical examinations at Ellis Island, also began to argue that many immigrants were "inferior."

The government sent Laughlin to research his theories in Europe. In 1924, he returned and spoke before Congress in support of immigration restrictions on the number of non-European and Eastern-European immigrants.

"America must remain American"

The Immigration Restriction Act of 1924 created a strict quota system specifically aimed at slowing the flow of Italians and Jews who were coming in record numbers. Eugenics followers argued that these groups were inferior to those of Anglo-Saxon and northern European descent. Upon signing the new law, President Calvin Coolidge commented, "America must remain American." This phrase became popular with anti-immigration groups.

While Franklin D. Roosevelt was president from 1933 to 1945, the quota system blocked many Jews from escaping Germany. In addition, Great Britain refused to ease limits on Jewish immigration to Palestine (present-day Israel). Beginning in 1944, greater efforts were made to save threatened Jews. Sadly, the Holocaust was already well under way, and these actions were mostly too little and too late.

Immigration restrictions become hotly argued issues even today when wars or campaigns of hatred threaten people of other nations. Should refugees fleeing such conditions be allowed asylum in the United States when they manage to escape?

Workers stand in line to receive bread during the Great Depression. Workers such as these would soon organize themselves into unions to keep their jobs.

"Birds of passage" and labor unions

Not all immigrants dreamed of making a new life in America. So-called "birds of passage" came only to earn money to take back home to waiting families. Between 1880 and 1920, only about half of the immigrants from Italy, Poland, Greece, and other countries of eastern and central Europe became U.S. citizens.

Because their future was not in the United States, such workers tended not to support unions. Unions required membership fees, and "birds of passage" wanted simply to take home as much money as possible. When World War I began in 1914, however, fewer immigrants were interested in returning to Europe. Support for unions rose. Still, conflict was common between new and established American workers.

The steelworkers' strike of 1919 is one example. When 250,000 unskilled immigrant steelworkers in Indiana and Pennsylvania struck for safer working conditions, higher wages, and unions, skilled workers refused to support them. These skilled, more established workers usually saw immigrant workers as inferior. The striking immigrants showed prejudice, too, not allowing African-Americans to join them. This was a mistake, because African-American workers from the rural South eventually broke the strike.

Such splits based on ethnicity, race, and skill level prevented the growth of unions until the 1930s. When the Great Depression came, workers of all nationalities united to protect jobs and their standard of living.

Jews Flee Pogroms and the Holocaust

Prejudice in Europe

During the late 1800s and 1900s, European Jews were the largest group to enter the United States. In 1907 alone, 258,000 Jews came. Most came for economic opportunities, but the wish to escape from anti-Jewish prejudice was often a motivation.

In 1881, a Jewish terrorist assassinated Russia's Czar, Alexander II. Anti-Jewish riots occurred across Russia. Jewish homes were destroyed, and Jews were attacked, beaten, or murdered. The Russian government began to more strictly enforce laws that required Jews to live within the Pale, an area along the border with Germany and the Austro-Hungarian Empire. A law passed in 1882 banning Jews from becoming farmers, industrial workers, doctors, lawyers, teachers, or from holding public office. Jews were also banned from many schools.

At the same time, in Poland and Russia as well as other Eastern European nations, *pogroms* were common. These were anti-Jewish riots and massacres which often took place with government participation.

At the time this photo was taken in 1935, signs like this had begun to appear all over Germany. It says "Jews not wanted in this place!"

Hitler's hate targets Jews

Adolph Hitler's hatred for Jews was clear long before World War II. He blamed Jews for all of Germany's economic troubles after World War I. After he became dictator, he soon declared he wanted to deport all of Germany's Jews to any countries that would have them. But the U.S., Canada, and Great Britain did little to save them. The United States would not increase the number of Jewish immigrants allowed to enter the United States each year under the quota system established by the Immigration Restriction Act in 1924.

Mass violence against German Jews broke out on November 9 and 10, 1938. Jewish businesses and synagogues throughout Germany were burned and smashed, which is why the event became known as Kristallnacht (the "Night of Broken Glass"). Many Jews who could afford to emigrate and who received permission left for the United States.

18

Hitler's Nazi Germany eventually desired not to deport Jews, but to kill them. Mobile killing units and concentration camps established by the Nazis in World War II eventually killed six million Jews, an event that has come to be called the Holocaust.

Germany's defeat in World War II did not put an end to pogroms. In Kielce, Poland, mobs attacked Jews after false rumors spread that Jews were using the blood of Christian children for ceremonies. Forty-two Jews were killed and about fifty were wounded.

The pogrom in Kielce led to hundreds of thousands of Holocaust survivors fearing for their lives again. Jews from Poland and other countries of eastern Europe headed to displaced persons camps that had been established in Germany, Austria, and Italy at the end of the war. Many ended up in the United States.

Hitler at a Nazi rally in Dortmann, Germany, in the 1930s. The Western world offered Jews little help to escape from Hitler's crazed hatred.

Jewish success in the United States

From the first Jewish immigrants permitted entrance in the late 1800s to Holocaust survivors after World War II, Jews in the United States have flourished. Many started by working as peddlers, shopkeepers, tailors, or shoemakers. Jewish immigrants helped create the Hollywood film industry in the 1910s and 1920s and have contributed greatly to medical progress.

Immigrants Escape Homeland Troubles

German immigrants settle the Midwest

According to the 2000 United States census, 46.5 million Americans claim German ancestry—over 10 million more than any other group. The roots were planted in the mid-1800s. Between 1840 and 1890, four million Germans came to the United States.

Rather than a single disaster such as the Irish Potato Famine, a series of political and economic troubles sent Germans and other northern and western Europeans to the United States. Thousands of German farmers were forced to move as the Industrial Revolution continued to change Europe. Many Germans also came following a failed popular revolution in 1848. Disappointed German patriots who had hoped to bring democracy to Germany headed for the U.S.

Other disappointed revolutionaries from Italy, Ireland, Poland, and Austria-Hungary also left Europe.The Homestead Act passed by Congress in 1862 gave free land to those willing to settle in the Midwest. German immigrants helped settle what would become Chicago, St. Louis, Milwaukee, Cincinnati, and Germantown, Pennsylvania. Over 50 percent of the residents of Wisconsin claim German ancestry.

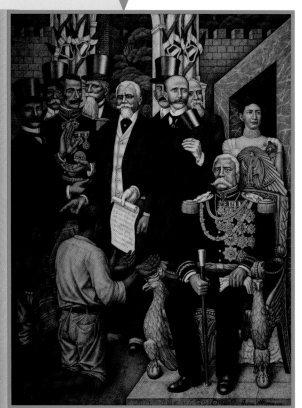

A painting of Mexican dictator Diaz and his wealthy associates with poor Mexican peasants asking for help.

Like German immigrant farmers, Germans from Berlin and other big cities also tended to go west. But unlike most new immigrants, few Germans were forced to work as unskilled laborers. They became bakers, tailors, shoemakers, brewers, butchers, and opticians. Skilled German tradesmen later were often leaders of labor unions across the growing United States.

Immigration from Mexico

The United States took over almost half of Mexico through war and land purchases between 1845 and 1854. As a result, more than 80,000 Mexicans "immigrated" without going anywhere.

Since then, political trouble in Mexico and economic opportunity in the United States have caused many Mexicans to immigrate. The majority entered the country legally. Others have illegally crossed the 2,000-mile border between the two countries.

Much of the earliest Mexican immigration occurred during the reign of Porfirio Diaz from 1876 to 1911. Diaz and his friends controlled most of Mexico's wealth. Peasants working on the land never earned much, while the cost of food and housing continued to rise. Many fled to the United States to seek a better life. During the revolution of 1910, still more fled.

Since the 1800s, Mexicans have crossed the border legally and illegally to work as farm laborers. They pick fruit on the farms and in the orchards of California and other states. Often, entire families work hard together for little money and live in uncomfortable or even unhealthful conditions. They suffer prejudice and even violent attacks from Americans who believe that Mexicans will eventually take their jobs or harm their way of life. Many Mexican immigrants have succeeded, however, especially throughout the Southwest.

Armenia: the 20th century's first genocide

Armenians once lived in the mountainous region between Turkey and Russia. They were part of an ancient civilization built in the territory where the Bible says Noah's Ark landed. Armenians have their own language, alphabet, religions, and customs.

Armenia was long ruled by the Ottoman Empire, of which Turkey was the center. In World War I, Russia fought Turkey, and Armenians volunteered to help the Russian army. Turkey responded by killing as many as 1.5 million Armenians between 1915 and 1923. Many of those who escaped the killing immigrated to the United States. Today, there are more than 800,000 Armenian-Americans. Many have settled in California, particularly in San Francisco, Los Angeles and Fresno.

Some of the Armenians killed by the Turks in 1919. Many Armenians fled to the United States in order to survive.

World Turmoil Modifies Immigration, 1930s to 1952

Depression leads to war

The Great Depression greatly harmed economies around the world. Poverty and hunger became worldwide problems. The United States suffered, too. The U.S. economy failed, and jobs grew nearly impossible to find. As a result, immigration fell.

The United States, Europe, and Asia soon moved from economic depression into World War II. Germany, under dictator Adolph Hitler, joined with Japan and Italy in hopes of taking over other countries. Great Britain, France, China, the United States, Canada, Australia, and eventually the Soviet Union opposed them.

This is a Japanese internment camp in California during World War II. The U.S. government did not intern German or Italian descendants.

With war starting in Europe, many German and Italian Americans were detained and questioned by the United States government to find possible spies. But truly shameful treatment was reserved for Japanese Americans, even though they were also legal immigrants or born in the United States.

Japanese American internment

Following the Japanese attack on Pearl Harbor in 1941, President Roosevelt declared war on Japan and Germany. He also announced Executive Order 9066, which, for national defense, permitted the military to ignore some of the constitutional rights of American citizens.

As a result, 120,000 Japanese and Japanese Americans living on the west coast were forced to leave their homes and jobs. They were interned in what President Roosevelt called "concentration camps." Half of those held were children. Although many Japanese families had been U.S. citizens for several generations, they were interned, surrounded by barbed wire and armed guards, for as long as four years. In some cases family members were even separated and put into different camps. The U.S. government claimed what it did was necessary to avoid possible sabotage or spying. But Americans of German or Italian descent were not interned.

In 1988, Congress passed the Civil Liberties Act of 1988. The act acknowledged that "a grave injustice was done" to those interned. Victims of internment were each given $20,000 to compensate them. The check from the U.S. government was sent with a signed apology from the president speaking for the American people.

Displaced persons

Displaced persons were those left homeless following World War II. Countless cities and villages had been destroyed, civilians and soldiers had died, and six million Jews and two million other people targeted by the Nazis had been murdered. As a result, the world was left with more refugees than it could handle.

Money cannot heal all effects

Although the official apology in 1988 was greatly appreciated by Japanese American leaders, it could not heal the emotional and physical problems of all victims. Heart disease and early death are twice as common in former internees as in Japanese Americans who were not placed in the camps.

The S.S. Marine Flasher *arrives in New York on May 20, 1946, carrying more than 800 displaced persons. Many of them were orphans who had lost parents in Nazi concentration camps.*

The greatest difficulties were faced by Holocaust survivors. From 1945 to 1952, more than 250,000 Jewish displaced persons lived in camps as well as in cities in Germany, Austria, and Italy. These displaced persons camps were often established inside the former concentration camps. But where would all of these people live? They could not return to destroyed homes and villages.

Under strong pressure from Jewish Americans, President Harry S Truman took an active interest in assisting survivors. In 1948, he signed the Displaced Persons Act. The new law allowed 100,000 refugees to immigrate to the United States over a four-year period. The act was amended in 1950 to make immigration easier for survivors. Most survivors settled in Israel or the United States. In all, the United States accepted 395,000 refugees from countries affected by the war.

Cold War Refugees, 1945–1965

The communist threat

After Nazi Germany, Italy, and Japan were defeated in World War II, the United States had a new enemy: communism as supported by the Union of Soviet Socialist Republics (USSR). The two superpowers never actually fought with bullets and bombs, but their struggle to dominate world events came to be called the Cold War.

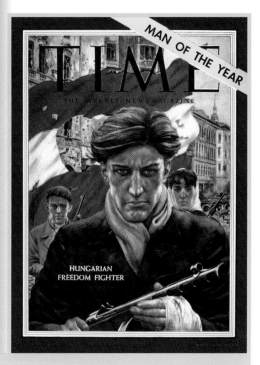

HUNGARIAN
FREEDOM FIGHTER

TIME's Man of the Year

TIME is a weekly newsmagazine read by millions of Americans. It is the most widely read newsmagazine in the United States. At the end of every year, it selects a person or people who it believes had the biggest influence on the year's events. Very often the people did something especially courageous and noble. For 1956, TIME chose the Hungarian freedom fighter as its Man of the Year.

This war, like World Wars I and II, created refugees. U.S. officials came to view immigration as one possible way to fight communism. A number of new laws allowed more people fleeing communist governments to settle in the United States. Often, these people were thinkers and scientists. The Soviet Union hesitated to let such people emigrate for various reasons. Some knew too much about national secrets and military matters. Also, the Soviet leadership feared a "brain drain" would weaken the country.

In 1953, Congress passed the Refugee Relief Act. The act allowed more than 200,000 people escaping from communist nations to immigrate to the United States. These extra immigrants did not count against the quotas established by previous laws.

Hungarian freedom fighters

Following World War II, the USSR took over the nations of Eastern Europe. The USSR set up communist governments which they then ruled by persuasion or, when necessary, force. On October 23, 1956, a group of students in Hungary held a demonstration in the capital city of Budapest. They demanded that Hungary be freed from Soviet domination. They wanted to end communism and start democracy in Hungary.

Soon, the students attempted to take over the city's radio station to spread their message. Hungarian police released tear gas to break up the crowds. When the students did not run away, police began beating and arresting them. The angry crowd soon attacked police in hopes of freeing those arrested. The police fired upon the crowds. A revolution had begun.

Hungarians look at a statue of Soviet dictator Joseph Stalin pulled down during the Hungarian Revolution. Later, they smashed it to pieces.

During the night, Soviet troops moved in to stop the revolt. But rather than stopping the violence, the arrival of Soviet forces spread fighting to other parts of the country. People calling themselves "freedom fighters" took over factories, Soviet weapons warehouses, and even Soviet tanks.

Encouraged by their successes and by supportive broadcasts from Radio Free Europe and the Voice of America, Hungarians battled Soviet soldiers. The Soviets pulled back and Hungarians started setting up a new government. Hungarians celebrated their victory over the mighty USSR.

But it was a temporary victory. More Soviet forces came and Hungarian resistance was defeated. Many of the leaders of the revolt were executed by firing squads. Thousands died in the fighting, and many more were jailed. More than 200,000 people fled the country.

Bravery finds a home

Americans had hoped the Hungarian Revolution would succeed and were saddened when it did not. About 38,000 Hungarians from the failed revolution were allowed to enter the United States. Even those Americans usually opposed to immigration gave their support.

Cubans Flee Castro

Wealthy not welcome in communism

The Cuban Revolution of 1959 ended the long reign of dictator Fulgencio Batista and put Fidel Castro in charge. Most Cubans were pleased with the change. Castro's policies were communist and generally aimed at taking money from the rich and giving it to the poor. Wealthy and educated Cubans sought to escape with their possessions. More than 150,000 middle class, pro-Batista, and anticommunist Cubans soon left the country. Since Castro rose to power, more than 800,000 Cubans have come to the United States. The majority have settled in Miami—one area of the city is called "Little Havana" after the Cuban capital—and other Florida cities.

The Cuban leader Fidel Castro gives a speech in 1960.

Because many of the Cubans who originally fled were well educated and fairly rich, the Cuban community in south Florida flourished. They have become powerful politically and pressure the U.S. government to be hostile toward Castro's government. The United States refuses to trade with Cuba or to allow most travel to and from the island.

Escape in the 1980s

During the 1980s, immigration became the focus of U.S.-Cuban relations. In April of 1980, around 10,000 Cubans forced their way into the Peruvian embassy in Havana, Cuba's capital. They wanted asylum from Castro's government. Castro allowed 125,000 Cubans to board boats of every shape and size and leave the port of Mariel bound for the United States. The incident broke U.S. immigration laws, and this wave of illegal immigrants angered the United States.

Among the willing emigrants, Castro had placed some criminals and mental patients, further angering U.S. officials. They banned all Cuban immigration. After arguing awhile, the United States and Cuba agreed to resume normal immigration.

In August 1994, another wave of Cuban immigrants came. Cubans marched to protest food shortages and frequent electricity blackouts. The Cuban government responded by allowing 30,000 more Cubans to set sail for the United States. Many would-be immigrants traveled in unsafe boats and on rafts. A number of Cubans drowned before reaching Florida. Again, the United States grew angry with Castro.

Child causes immigration law tug-of-war

Six-year old Elian Gonzalez became a symbol of the struggle between those in the United States who wish to cut off communist Cuba and those who want to accept that Castro is in charge and attempt to work with him.

In November of 1999 a boat carrying Elian and his mother sank while trying to reach Florida. Elian's mother drowned. His father, still living in Cuba, wanted the boy returned to Cuba. But some of Elian's relatives in Florida refused to return him to what they believed was life without freedom in Cuba. What was U.S. immigration law in this case?

Elian's father saw the Miami relatives as kidnappers. The relatives and their anti-Castro, Cuban-American supporters believed that Elian's mother had given her life to bring her son to freedom and that such a dying wish should be honored.

News organizations sent the story around the world. The Miami relatives loudly disobeyed the U.S. government, which believed it had to reunite Elian with his father. Finally, U.S. authorities took Elian from the Miami relatives' house and returned him to his father in Havana, where he received a hero's welcome.

The Haitian Refugee Crisis

Family dictators

From 1991 through 1994, a bad situation grew worse in the Caribbean nation of Haiti, the poorest nation in the Western Hemisphere. Haitians had suffered for decades under the murderous dictatorship of their president, Papa Doc Duvalier. Papa Doc was followed by his son, Baby Doc, and by a series of cruel and dishonest military governments. Those who dared to criticize the government often were found dead as a warning to others.

Large numbers of Haitian refugees had begun arriving in the United States by boat as early as 1972. They hoped to escape the Duvalier dictatorship and its secret police. These so-called "boat people" often traveled in unsteady or dangerously overloaded boats. Many overturned or sank, leading to hundreds of deaths. Crooked smugglers often abused and sometimes even killed Haitians who had hired them to carry them to the United States.

This picture shows Baby Doc Duvalier and his father, Papa Doc Duvalier, behind him. Their cruel administration caused many Haitians to attempt immigration.

Those who made it to the United States were not welcomed. At U.S. Immigration Service investigations, lawyers for Haitian boat people regularly asked for political asylum. The government generally decided that such refugees were trying to enter the United States for economic reasons, which they would not permit. These illegal immigrants were returned to Haiti, where they were often severely punished or killed.

New policy of temporary asylum

U.S. policy shifted in 1980 when President Jimmy Carter faced huge arrivals of both Haitian and Cuban refugees at the same time. Carter decided that the United States had no right to treat the two refugee groups differently. Each was fleeing a repressive government.

But instead of simply giving asylum to both Haitians and Cubans, Carter created a new immigration classification. 18,000 Haitians and 125,000 Cubans were given "temporary asylum."

In 1981, President Ronald Reagan shifted U.S. policy again. He ordered Coast Guard ships to stop Haitian boats before they reached shore. This removed the need for immigration hearings, because would-be illegal immigrants never reached U.S. soil. Reagan also announced that Haitians who escaped the Coast Guard and landed in the United States would be held for a long time in federal prisons and Immigration and Naturalization Service detention centers. 433 boats were caught and 25,551 Haitians were forced to return to Haiti between 1981 and 1991.

Haitian refugees sail into Biscayne Bay, Florida, in 1981.

The 1990s and democracy

When democracy came to Haiti in 1991, refugee numbers dropped sharply. But later in 1991, the military removed the elected president, Jean-Bertrand Aristide. Many people fled to the mountains or to neighboring Dominican Republic. More than 38,000 Haitians left the island and headed for the United States.

The United States was at first unwilling to send home these Haitians. President George H.W. Bush's administration decided to establish a Haitian refugee camp at a military base in the Caribbean. After the camp quickly filled up with 12,000 refugees, Bush ordered the immediate return of all additional Haitians picked up at sea.

When President Bill Clinton took office in 1993, he inherited the continuing problem of Haitians trying to escape their homeland. He did not have many options for controlling the problem, so the president decided to work to restore democratic government to Haiti. Discussions with Haiti's military government produced no results, so finally a U.S. military invasion in September of 1994 returned Jean-Bertrand Aristide to power. Freed from political terror, Haitians stopped trying to emigrate illegally by boat.

The United States and the United Nations have invested hundreds of millions of dollars in Haiti. Haiti's history from the mid-1900s shows that any emergencies in a nation close to the United States result in an immediate rise in legal and illegal immigration.

Modern Developments

Needed: immigrant doctors

Foreign-born doctors have treated countless American patients. They are more important than ever to healthcare in this country. Eutaw, Alabama, is one example. A poor town, it had trouble drawing American doctors to work there. This country town in the Deep South now depends on three doctors who came to the United States from Pakistan and one who came from the Philippines.

Local residents had worried that the county's small hospital would close. One of the Pakistanis, Dr. Adnan Seljuki, helps keep it open. He is impressed that although the town is poor, the healthcare is generally very good. Any patient who comes to the emergency room gets the best care available, he says.

Doctors such as these symbolize the effect of immigration on the U.S. medical world. Two of the three are immigrants, the one on the left from Asia, and the one on the right from East India.

Fitting in

Like immigrants of the past, the four doctors in Eutaw have done their best to communicate well in English. These doctors also have had to work to fit into the town's social life. Since they are Muslims in a mostly Christian town, and foreign-born in a place where most people's families have farmed the land for generations, this has sometimes been difficult.

Rural areas are not the only places needing foreign doctors. Foreign-born doctors help at large city hospitals, too. In the U.S., approximately 16,000 to 17,000 medical students graduate from medical schools each year and become what are called residents. But the nation's hospitals need about 22,000 first-year residents. Today, 5,000 to 6,000 residents every year are immigrants.

Community spirit

One kind of visa issued by the U.S. government requires foreign doctors to work for two to four years in areas short of doctors, such as Eutaw, Alabama. The doctors are then usually granted permanent work visas.

Usually foreign doctors leave rural America after finishing the time necessary for their visa. But Eutaw's three Pakistani doctors decided to remain there even after they were free to leave. They felt welcome in the town. The doctors, all strong Muslims, were especially pleased that their patients showed them strong support following the terrorist attacks of September 11, 2001, which were carried out by Muslim extremists.

Opponents of Proposition 187 protest in California in this 1994 photo.

Proposition 187

In 1994, 59 percent of California voters approved Proposition 187. The measure banned illegal immigrants from receiving government aid money. It also banned children who were illegal immigrants from public schools and universities, and prevented them from using government-funded medical care. Opponents of Proposition 187 immediately went to court and temporarily stopped the changes. But this did not silence the 4.6 million California voters who had said they were tired of illegal immigrants. Proposition 187 sent a powerful message.

Some of these voters opposed only illegal immigration. But many likely wanted to slow or stop immigration altogether. Such feelings may grow stronger as immigration continues. Throughout the 1990s, immigration added more than a million people a year to the U.S. population. By 1994, 9 percent of the U.S. population was born elsewhere. That is nearly twice the percentage of foreign-born people living in the United States in 1970.

A question of change

A reporter visited a government services center in 1992 to write about immigration in California. There he met a woman who was surprised by the changes immigration had brought to her state. No one else visiting the center was speaking English, leading her to wonder, "Is this still the United States of America?"

Melting Pot or Quilt? 1965–2003

Immigration continues . . .

As of March 2003, 33.1 million legal and illegal immigrants lived in the United States. Here are a few facts about immigration today:

Neither the recent slowing of the U.S. economy nor the terrorist attacks of September 11, 2001, have reduced the rate of immigration. More than 3.3 million legal and illegal immigrants have entered the country since January 2000.

About 33.1 million immigrants are living in the United States, which is about 11 percent of the population. But at the peak of the enormous wave of immigration in 1910, the number of immigrants living in the United States was a little over 14 percent of the population.

The Manhattan area of New York City after the terrorist attacks on September 11, 2001.

. . . but changes come

Each year 1.5 million immigrants come to the U.S. and about 750,000 children are born to immigrant women, which means that the U.S. population grows by over 2 million people each year. Two-thirds of U.S. population growth is based on those factors.

The world is different from just a few years ago. Many Americans and government officials are ready to refuse immigration to many because of the danger of international terrorism. Many immigrants from the Arab world have been held and questioned for long periods of time without being charged with any crime. Some Americans think this is necessary to remain safe. Others worry that such treatment is unfair and racist.

The way many U.S. immigrants choose to live upon arriving in the U.S. has also changed. During the first waves of immigration in the late 1800s and early 1900s, the United States was often called a "melting pot." Immigrants from all over the world abandoned most of their native customs and languages. To quickly blend in with U.S. society, they adopted a completely American way of life.

Today, some people think of the United States more like a giant quilt. Rather than melting into a homogeneous United States, immigrants often keep many of their customs and ways of life. They may cluster in neighborhoods where their native language is spoken and make little effort to "fit in." They are part of America, but like a quilt, each part preserves its unique character. It is hard to say which approach is best for the whole nation.

Immigration and September 11, 2001

The list of victims of the terrorist attacks in New York City and Washington D.C. included immigrants from every continent and region of the world. The attacks by a group of Muslim extremists from the Middle East also scared Muslims and Arab Americans into thinking that they might be targeted for hatred and crimes of revenge.

In Arizona, such a crime happened. A gas station owner named Balbir Singh Sodhi was shot to death on September 15th, 2001. Sodhi was a Sikh from India. Like most Sikh men, he had a long beard and wore a turban. Sikhs have no connection to the Arab world or Islam. But the killer had believed so. When news of the murder spread, Americans were quick to condemn not only this senseless crime, but also hatred of the world's countless innocent Muslims. More than 3,000 people of all religions and nationalities attended Sodhi's funeral.

Sikhs protest shortly after the September 11, 2001, terrorist attacks. The Sikhs protested against terrorism and against prejudice from those who mistakenly believed they were Muslims.

Somalis Escape Hunger and Terror

Civil war

In 1992, the United States led a United Nations peacekeeping mission in Somalia, an eastern African nation that has often suffered from war. A civil war had cut off supplies. Troops planned to protect aid workers distributing food to the starving population.

Some Somalis emigrated to escape. Sherwa Musse is one. At age 13, he saw his mother and younger brother killed. Following his mother's death, Shera's father took him and his four brothers and sisters to refugee camps in Yemen, Ethiopia, and Kenya before finally being admitted to the United States in January 1996. He lived in three states before he graduated from high school and attended college. He moved to Lewiston, Maine, in March 2001 with his wife.

A Somali woman walks in the streets of Lewiston, Maine.

Musse chose Lewiston because he had heard good things about it from other Somali refugees. Somalis had flocked there in search of work and a community of fellow Somalis. He found a job and was happy with his decision. He usually felt welcome in the town.

Limits to welcoming?

But in January of 2002, Lewiston's mayor wrote an open letter to Somali elders asking them to "reduce the stress on our limited finances and our generosity." The letter said that Lewiston had done everything it could, "financially, physically, and emotionally" because more than 1,000 Somalis had moved there since February 2001. The letter suggested that Somalis were receiving too much government aid and that no more Somalis should come to Lewiston for a while.

Are they 'immigrants'? No—they're workers!

"Some people ask why we hire Somalis," says a manager of a printing company in Lewiston where Musse works. *"If they have the work experience and they interview well, they're in. It has nothing to do with the color of their skin or where they come from. Somalis have proven to be good workers and very dependable."*

The mayor's letter hurt Somalis. Many long-time Lewiston residents were also upset with the mayor. A local Christian church held a friendship walk to the mosque to show support for Somalis. The mayor met with Somali leaders and told them he was "deeply concerned" that so many people misunderstood the purpose of his letter.

Musse was offended by the letter. He and his wife saw themselves as hardworking, contributing members of the Lewiston community. "Since I've been here, I've been working," Musse said. "The mayor sounds like we're all completely dependent on government help, but most Somali people aren't like that."

Not all Lewiston community members were supportive of Somalis. Some citizens thought that Lewiston was changing too quickly. Rumors claimed that Somalis were receiving free housing, extra economic help, and even free cars. Although local officials said Somali immigrants got only what was available to any low-income resident, some people simply did not want to give tax money to help newcomers.

Somali women talk with a longtime woman resident of Lewiston, Maine, at a "Meet the Immigrants" evening.

Reaching understanding

City officials said Lewiston simply could not continue to pay for the needs of any more than the 1,000 Somali immigrants already living in Lewiston. Somali leaders and city officials recognized that some Somalis were getting government assistance that ranged from free school lunch to medical care. But many Somalis were not getting help.

The presence of Somalis did lead to business opportunities. One poultry processing plant reopened and hired twelve Somalis to help them produce chicken that is *halal* (butchered in the Muslim tradition). The company hopes to expand and sell *halal* chicken throughout the East Coast.

Despite the trouble, Sherwa Musse and many Somalis continued to believe that Lewiston was a good place. He appreciated the chance that immigration gave him for education and work in the United States.

Desperate to Come to the United States

Risking one's life

It might be hard for native-born Americans to imagine how desperately some people wish to come to the United States. Mexicans risk their lives under a blazing desert sun, hoping to sneak across the border. Cubans and Haitians have only rafts and tiny boats to cross rough seas to Florida.

Chinese smugglers found a new way to sneak illegal immigrants into the United States. In January 2000, two Chinese men were arrested in Seattle for trying to smuggle twelve other Chinese into the U.S. They had arranged to place the twelve inside a cargo container on a ship traveling from Hong Kong. The two men who made the arrangements, Yu Zheng and Sheng Ding, were illegal immigrants themselves. Authorities caught them waiting in a van parked at the Port of Seattle. The two men charged up to $60,000 for each person smuggled inside the container. By the time the container was unloaded, it was filthy.

Deadly cargo

The Seattle arrests led to discovery of more than 100 Chinese hidden inside similar containers aboard ships that had come to California, Washington, and Vancouver, British Columbia. The first twelve stowaways found were luckier than others. Smugglers care little about what might happen to smuggled people, and in one case, a tragedy

A cargo container ship sits in a Seattle dock on January 3, 2000, after twelve Chinese men were found hiding in a container.

resulted. Just a few days after officials in Seattle found the twelve stowaways, they made another discovery. On another ship from Hong Kong, eighteen stowaways were found in a container. Three had died during the long trip across the Pacific Ocean, and seven more needed to be hospitalized. In a ship at Vancouver, a group of smuggled Chinese were found locked in a dark steel container. They were using buckets for toilets, a small generator for power, and stored water and food to stay alive.

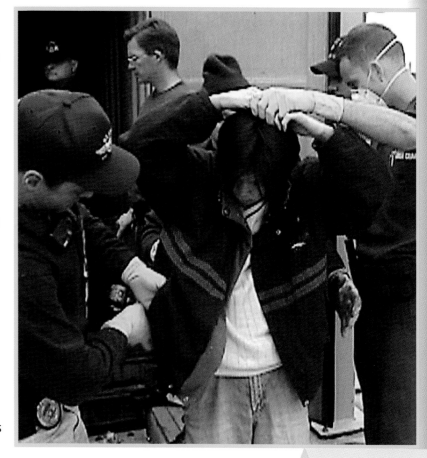

Shipping and customs officials say there is no way they can search every container shipped into the United States. It simply would not be practical. Officials now target those with soft canvas tops. These are used because air can reach the people hidden inside.

Police and Coast Guard officers search a Chinese immigrant caught in a ship's container on February 4, 1999. This man and ten others were lucky to have survived with good health.

One Chinese immigrant's story

Sui-Ming Tam came to the United States more than a decade before emigrants from China began hiding aboard container ships. Tam hid in the mountains for thirteen days, then swam across a bay filled with sharks to reach Hong Kong. Once in Hong Kong, he waited five more years to find someone in the United States who would sponsor him as a worker. He had to work for the people two years and pay them $400 a month. He is now a U.S. citizen and operates a noodle-manufacturing company in Seattle's Chinatown.

Tam knows that coming to the United States and working is much harder than what people hear in China. He thinks too many Chinese believe wild stories about American riches—that the United States is a "mountain of gold." He says those thinking about trying to immigrate to the United States should know about the hardships.

Female Immigrant Success Stories

Americans do not always know about the economic contribution of immigrants. But census information shows that immigrants boldly start businesses of all types. Immigrants are risk-takers. Highly skilled immigrants helped make the U.S. economy grow fast in the 1990s. They started companies that have become giants such as Intel and Sun Microsystems.

In addition, more and more women have become business owners. Women own more than 5.4 million businesses in the United States. Immigrant women—especially Koreans, Greeks, Taiwanese, and Iranians—own businesses at a higher rate than native-born Americans.

Immigrant women often run small shops, but others work to establish themselves among high-tech companies. Either way, immigrant women are writing their own American story.

Caroline Mulligan from Ireland

Caroline Mulligan left Ireland at age 21 in 1991. From the time she was a little girl, Ms. Mulligan wanted to go to the United States. Today she owns a hair salon in a fancy part of Boston.

Mulligan was trained in Ireland and planned to work for a beauty shop in Boston after she immigrated. But after arriving, she found that no shop would hire her because she did not already have her own regular customers. Some shops offered her low-paying work as an apprentice, but she was already a fully trained stylist.

She finally found work and cut hair next to another stylist named Cheri O'Donnell, a third-generation Irish-American. Together, they dreamed of opening their own shop.

In December 1999, they did just that. They now employ four stylists, have about 800 regular customers, and are even busier than they had hoped. Mulligan says becoming a successful American was hard work but very rewarding.

Yolanda Zambrano from Colombia

Zambrano studied accounting at night in Colombia, where she worked at a travel agency during the day. Her plan was to finish school in the United States and become an accountant. She did not speak English when she came to the United States in 1990 and married her Colombian boyfriend. In an effort to improve her English, she volunteered at a nearby travel agency. One day the owner told her he was tired of the business and suggested she buy it from him.

She had never imagined starting her own business. Although she only had $2,000 in savings, she decided to do it. There were many problems, and at first she did not know about available help for immigrants. She eventually got a small loan and the necessary $20,000 for a business license. She hired and trained a bilingual staff and worked on attracting both Spanish- and English-speaking customers.

Zambrano's agency has grown from earning $100,000 in 1990 to $7 million in sales in 2001. It arranges travel all over the world while specializing in trips to Latin America and the Caribbean. Success has come, she says, by focusing on the goal and taking advantage of the opportunities in the United States. Zambrano is now a proud and happy U.S. citizen.

Vietnam and the Boat People

War's end causes immigration

Starting in the 1960s, the United States fought in the Vietnam War in an attempt to stop communist North Vietnam from taking over South Vietnam. About 58,000 Americans and over one million Vietnamese died in the war, which ended in 1975. When the U.S. finally left Vietnam, many high-ranking South Vietnamese military and government officials and their families were evacuated by airplane, helicopter, and ship.

By the end of May 1975, the U.S. military had transported 120,000 Vietnamese along with 5,500 Cambodians and Laotians to four military bases. These refugees were part of the largest resettlement program in U.S. history. But so many refugees could not be settled instantly. Those who had at least $4,000 per family member were soon permitted to leave the bases and find homes. The rest waited for American families, religious groups, or companies to sponsor them.

South Vietnamese try to scale the wall of the U.S. Embassy in Saigon on April 29, 1975. With the war nearly lost, they feared communist North Vietnamese rule.

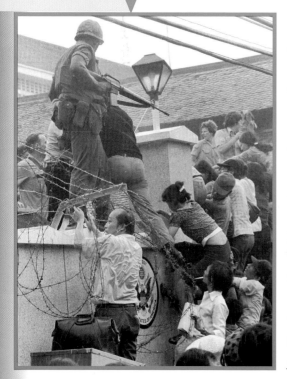

Immigration officials decided to evenly distribute these needy refugees across the country. The policy meant that a few Vietnamese families found themselves alone in rural Alaska!

Divided by experience

Vietnam is a country of many different cultures, languages, religions, and traditions. But in the United States, divisions among Vietnamese are between those who were evacuated by the United States at the war's end and those who were not. The relatives of South Vietnamese officials and military men who were left behind suffered. Because educated and democratic-minded people were a threat to North Vietnamese rule of the south, most were arrested and "re-educated" in jungle camps.

"I risked my life"

For many of the first boat people, especially teenagers and young adults, the trial of escape—30 percent of the boat people died at sea—made them strong and able to succeed. "I risked my life to come here," says Nam Nguyen, a Vietnamese who arrived in the United States as a twelve-year-old in 1979.

When to forgive and move ahead?

In 1994, President Bill Clinton took steps toward normal relations with Vietnam. Former prisoners are horrified that the United States might be friendly to the Vietnamese government that made them suffer. It is doubly upsetting for them that the Vietnamese Americans who escaped Saigon in 1975 also favor this. Younger Vietnamese American businesspeople also believe they can help their ancestral land grow. Who is right?

Eventually, the communist government closed the re-education camps and released their victims. These former political prisoners, more than 100,000, arrived in the United States as part of a special resettlement program. But they have had trouble adjusting to life in the United States and often remain poor for years as they work low-wage jobs or are unable to work at all. Many of the most successful Vietnamese are those who were evacuated from Saigon in 1975.

Vietnamese boat people

With the communists remaining in power, Vietnamese people have continued to immigrate to the United States. A second wave of refugees came to the United States in 1978. These "boat people" took to the sea in anything that floated. Most were ethnically Chinese. Many found support in the Chinatown districts of Chicago and Seattle.

Eventually, more boat people arrived who were mostly coastal fishermen. Because they owned their own boats, escape from Vietnam was relatively easy. These immigrants formed fishing communities along the Gulf Coast of Texas and neighboring states. They found success despite racial prejudice from other fishermen.

This is the outside of Asian Garden Mall in Westminster, California. Many Vietnamese immigrants settled in this area.

Later Vietnamese immigrants chose to settle throughout California. The booming California economy in the 1980s along with warm weather and generous public aid drew new immigrants of all kinds. Today, there are 700,000 Vietnamese Americans in the United States. That is nearly as many as Japanese, Korean, and Indian Americans.

Fighting Prejudice with Facts

Many Americans who oppose immigration or dislike immigrants do not have correct information. Here is a list of some common myths followed by the truth about immigration and immigrants.

Myth Number 1: Immigrants steal American jobs

Not true. Immigrants actually *create* jobs. They are more likely to be self-employed and start new businesses than are native-born Americans. Immigrants start around 18 percent of new small businesses each year, and small businesses create almost 80 percent of new jobs in the United States each year.

Myth Number 2: The United States has too many immigrants

Not true. In some states it may seem that way. Three-quarters of all immigrants entering the United States during the 1980s settled in just six states: California, New York, Texas, Florida, New Jersey, and Illinois. While the number of immigrants is larger than ever before, immigrants are generally a small percentage of the population. Also, less than 1.5 percent of the world's yearly refugee population comes to the United States.

Xenophobia (the fear of outsiders) may also contribute to wrong ideas about immigrant numbers. For a long time, the majority of immigrants were white Europeans. Those of more recent decades represent more races and countries. Also, recent immigrants often settle near each other in urban areas, making it seem there are more overall. In 1990, 93 percent of foreign-born Americans lived in metropolitan areas, compared with 73 percent of native-born Americans.

Myth Number 3: Immigrants are an economic burden

Not true. Immigrants earn $240 billion a year. They pay $90 billion a year in taxes while receiving $5 billion in aid. In fact, new immigrants must prove that they will not be a burden before they are allowed to enter the United States.

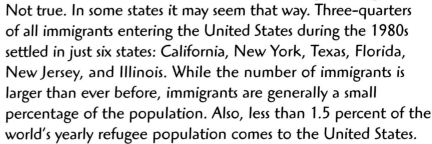

The Statue of Liberty, symbol of freedom and opportunity for many immigrants as they enter the United States.

Compared to the average native-born American, the normal immigrant is more likely to have a job or to start a new business and saves a greater percentage of his or her earnings. An immigrant of working age who has not come to this country as a refugee is less likely to need welfare than a native-born person.

Myth Number 4: Immigrants do not become part of American society

Not true. First- and second-generation immigrants often assimilate so quickly that their parents and grandparents fear they will lose their native culture. English classes do not have enough teachers for all the immigrants who want classes. After fifteen years in the United States, 75 percent of Spanish-speaking immigrants speak English regularly. The children of immigrants, although bilingual, overwhelmingly prefer English to their native language. Finally, one-third of immigrants and refugees marry outside their group.

Many positives

Studies have shown that most immigrant groups have strong family values. They tend to have more children than native born couples. Immigrants are also more likely to be married: 60 percent versus 55 percent. And only 8 percent of immigrants are divorced or separated versus 11 percent of natives.

Immigrants tend to value education greatly. Many come to the United States specifically for educational reasons. New Americans are just as likely as natives to hold a college degree and twice as likely to hold a Ph.D.

Immigrants respect the law as much, if not more, than native-born Americans. They are less likely than natives to be in prison.

Immigrants are important to the United States. They always have been. They keep the United States educated, fed, clothed, and safe. They value the goals and principles in the U.S. Constitution at least as much as the average native-born American. It should never be forgotten: immigration is part of the family history of every citizen of the United States.

About 300 new immigrants celebrate being sworn in as citizens of the United States at Elllis Island in May 1996.

Timeline

1619	Africans and Caribbeans are brought to North America to work as slaves
1760–1830	The Industrial Revolution in Great Britain forces many who were farm workers to look for new opportunities in the New World (North and South America)
1808	United States Congress bans the slave trade
1820	First Chinese immigrants arrive in California
1846	Potato famine in Ireland starts, causing 1.5 million Irish to immigrate to the United States by 1850
1849–1850	Immigrants from Latin America and China arrive for the California gold rush
1862	Congress passes the Homestead Act, which allows anyone willing to settle in the West to receive free land. Many immigrants take advantage of this.
1882	The Chinese Exclusion Act is passed, the only immigration legislation that targets a group only for racial reasons
1890	Steerage Act is passed, which places responsibility for passengers and crew on ships' captains
1892	Ellis Island opens in New York City, through which 75 percent of immigrants into the United States are admitted through 1924
1910	Angel Island opens
1924	The Immigration Restriction Act is passed to limit the number of non-Anglo Saxons immigrating into the United States
1941	Executive Order 9066 is passed, and 120,000 Japanese Americans are interned, from recent immigrants to second- and third-generation descendants
1948	The Displaced Persons Act permits survivors of Nazi Germany genocide to immigrate
1953	The Refugee Relief Act is passed, allowing more than 200,000 people over existing quotas to immigrate if they are escaping communism
1965	The Immigration and Nationality Act is passed, reducing immigration quotas
1975	The Vietnam War ends and many South Vietnamese immigrate to the United States
1980	In response to Cuban and Haitian boatpeople, President Carter creates "temporary asylum" status
1994	United States installs government in Haiti in effort to remove many Haitians' desire to emigrate
2001	Terrorists attack the United States, leading to more careful immigration restrictions and investigations

Some Famous Immigrants

Some of the people below also kept citizenship in their countries of birth. This status is called *dual citizenship*.

Artists
Mikhail Baryshnikov, dancer (Latvia)
I.M. Pei, architect of the Rock and Roll Hall of Fame (China)

Athletes
Mario Andretti, race car driver (Italy)
Bela Karolyi, Olympic gymnastic coach (Romania)
Martina Navratilova, tennis player (former Czechoslovakia)
Hakeem Olajuwon, basketball player (Nigeria)
Rafael Palmeiro, baseball player (Cuba)
Sammy Sosa, baseball player (Dominican Republic)

Authors
Isabel Allende, author *House of Spirits* (Peru - Chilean descent)
Frank McCourt, author *Angela's Ashes* (Ireland)
Elie Wiesel, Holocaust survivor, author, and Nobel Prize winner for Peace (Romania)

Entertainers
Dan Akroyd, actor (Canada)
Michael J. Fox, actor, *Back to the Future* (Canada)
Andy Garcia, actor (Cuba)
Bob Hope, comedian and actor (United Kingdom)
Selma Hyak, actor and film producer, *Frida* (Mexico)
Ang Lee, movie director, *The Hulk* (China)
Bela Lugosi, actor famous as Dracula (Hungary)
Ricardo Montalban, actor, *Fantasy Island* (Mexico)
Frank Oz, Muppet puppeteer (England)
Arnold Schwarzenegger, actor/bodybuilder (Austria)
William Shatner, actor famous as Captain Kirk of *Star Trek* (Canada)
Alex Trebek, game show host, *Jeopardy* (Canada)

Entrepreneurs
Andrew Grove, founder, Intel Corporation (Hungary)
Jenny Ming, Chief Executive Officer, Old Navy (Macau - China)
Pierre Omidyor, founder, E-Bay (India)

Fashion
Liz Claiborne, fashion designer (Belgium)
Iman, model and actress (Somalia)
Josie Natori, fashion designer (the Philippines)

Journalists
Peter Jennings, network television anchor (Canada)
Morley Safer, *60 Minutes* television journalist (Canada)

Politicians
Madeline Albright, former Secretary of State (Czechoslovakia)
Henry Kissinger, former Secretary of State (Germany)

Scientists
Albert Einstein, physicist and father of the Nuclear Age (Germany)
David Ho, AIDS researcher and *TIME* magazine's 1996 Man of the Year (Taiwan)

Singers, Songwriters, & Musicians
Placido Domingo, opera singer (Spain)
Gloria Estefan, singer/songwriter (Cuba)
Yo Yo Ma, concert cellist (France - China)
Carlos Santana, rock/jazz guitarist (Mexico)
Jon Secada, singer (Cuba)
Gene Simmons, rock musician, Kiss (Israel)
Eddie Van Halen, rock guitarist/musician (Netherlands)

Glossary

ancestor one from whom an individual is descended

apprentice person who promises for a period of time to work under someone and learn his or her trade

assimilate become part of something after joining it, in this case a country

asylum place of protection or shelter

bicentennial 200th anniversary

bilingual able to speak two languages

brain drain when too many talented and intelligent people leave a society

capitalism economic system in which ownership of land and wealth is mostly owned by individuals

cargo container big, strong box used to pack and store things on ships. Often as big as a house.

census count of the number of people in a city or country

communism social system in which property and goods are held in common

Czar name for the ruler of Russia until the Russian Revolution of 1917

deport force a person who is not a citizen to leave the country

detain hold or keep in as if in a prison

dictator person who rules with total authority, often cruelly

displaced persons camps places in Europe for refugees after World War II

dredge dig or gather, often from the bottom of a body of water

entrepreneur person who starts a business

eugenics belief that certain races are naturally different and often superior to others. Followers of eugenics wished to encourage or discourage birth, and to allow or ban immigration, based on this belief.

evacuate to remove people or troops from a place of danger

evict put out from property by legal action

extremist person whose beliefs are very different from the majority and center

famine general lack of food that leads to people starving

found establish, such as with a settlement or organization

genocide murder of nearly all members of a race or group

Great Depression 1930s in the United States, when the economy shrank and the unemployment rate was nearly 25 percent

Holocaust genocide of about six million Jews by Hitler's Nazi Germany

homogeneous of the same or similar type or nature

Industrial Revolution period in the late 1700s and early 1800s when machines started doing more work for people

infirmary place for the care and housing of sick people

intern force to stay within certain limits, especially during a war

invalidate weaken or destroy the effect of

Middle East region including Egypt, Saudi Arabia, Syria, Israel, Lebanon, Iraq, and Jordan

mosque Muslim building of worship

oath serious statement to God or some respected person or thing to witness to the truth of what the person says

platform statement of the beliefs for which a group or often a political party stands

proposition in elections, a possible law for which people vote yes or no directly

quota share or amount given to a group

repression being held down or held back by pressure

residency period of time an immigrant stays to establish that he or she lives in a country

resident doctor who has just graduated from medical school and works on a hospital staff to gain experience

sabotage damage or block a country's war effort

smuggle take out or bring in secretly

socialism system similar to communism, in which control of land, production and goods is held in common. In communism, the system is more widely established.

stowaway person who hides in a ship or airplane to travel for free

tolerate accept differences in others

tuberculosis disease in which fever, weakness, and fluid in lungs occur

turban long cloth that Sikhs wrap around their head

visa document that allows a traveler or immigrant to enter a country and stay for a period

warlord leader with many weapons in a country whose government is weak

welfare aid or money for poor, elderly, or disabled people

workhouse a kind of jail in the past where minor criminals were kept until their sentence was completed

Further Reading

Anderson, Dale. *Arriving at Ellis Island.* Milwaukee, Wisc.: Gareth Stevens, 2002.

Dudley, William. *Illegal Immigration.* Farmington Hills, Mich.: Gale Group, 2003.

Haberle, Susan E. *Jewish Immigrants, 1880–1924.* Minnetonka, Minn.: Capstone Press, 2002.

Hammerschmidt, Peter. *Land of Immigrants.* Broomall, Penn.: Mason Crest, 2002.

Perl, Lila. *To the Golden Mountain: The Chinese Who Built the Transcontinental Railroad.* Estes Park, Colo.: Benchmark Investigative Group, 2002.

Staff, Learning Links. *Immigration.* New Hyde Park, N.Y.: Learning Links, 2002.

Index